01/13

ANIMAL SAFARI

Antelopes

by Margo Gates

BELLWETHER MEDIA · MINNEAPOLIS, MN

Note to Librarians, Teachers, and Parents:

Blastoff! Readers are carefully developed by literacy experts and combine standards-based content with developmentally appropriate text.

Level 1 provides the most support through repetition of high-frequency words, light text, predictable sentence patterns, and strong visual support.

Level 2 offers early readers a bit more challenge through varied simple sentences, increased text load, and less repetition of high-frequency words.

Level 3 advances early-fluent readers toward fluency through increased text and concept load, less reliance on visuals, longer sentences, and more literary language.

Level 4 builds reading stamina by providing more text per page, increased use of punctuation, greater variation in sentence patterns, and increasingly challenging vocabulary.

Level 5 encourages children to move from "learning to read" to "reading to learn" by providing even more text, varied writing styles, and less familiar topics.

Whichever book is right for your reader, Blastoff! Readers are the perfect books to build confidence and encourage a love of reading that will last a lifetime!

This edition first published in 2014 by Bellwether Media, Inc.

No part of this publication may be reproduced in whole or in part without written permission of the publisher. For information regarding permission, write to Bellwether Media, Inc., Attention: Permissions Department, 5357 Penn Avenue South, Minneapolis, MN 55419.

Library of Congress Cataloging-in-Publication Data

Gates, Margo.
  Antelopes / by Margo Gates.
     p. cm. – (Blastoff! readers. Animal safari)
  Summary: "Developed by literacy experts for students in kindergarten through grade three, this book introduces antelopes to young readers through leveled text and related photos"– Provided by publisher.
  Audience: K to grade 3.
  Includes bibliographical references and index.
  ISBN 978-1-60014-907-8 (hardcover : alk. paper)
  1. Antelopes–Juvenile literature. I. Title. II. Series: Blastoff! readers. 1, Animal safari.
  QL737.U53G38 2014
  599.64–dc23
                                                                                    2013000885

Contents

What Are Antelopes?

Antelopes are **mammals** with **hooves**. Most live in dry grasslands.

hooves

Some antelopes
live in **deserts**.
Their wide hooves
help them walk
on sand.

Other antelopes
live on mountains.
Their hooves have
pads so they do
not slip.

Horns

All male antelopes
have horns. Most
females also
have horns.

Antelopes use their horns to fight lions and leopards. These animals are **predators**.

Male antelopes use their horns against one another. They fight for females and power.

Herds

Most antelopes
travel in **herds**.
They **graze**
on grasses and
other plants.

Staying Safe

Some females leave the herd to give birth. They hide their **calves** from predators.

Soon the calves
are ready to run
with the herd.
Antelopes must
stick together!

Glossary

calves—baby antelopes

deserts—dry lands with little rain

graze—to eat grasses and other plants

herds—groups of antelopes that travel together

hooves—hard coverings that protect the feet of some animals

mammals—warm-blooded animals that have backbones and feed their young milk

predators—animals that hunt other animals for food

To Learn More

AT THE LIBRARY

Borgert-Spaniol, Megan. *Gazelles.*
Minneapolis, Minn.: Bellwether Media, Inc.,
2013.

Gibbs, Maddie. *Antelope.* New York, N.Y.:
PowerKids Press, 2011.

Worth, Bonnie. *Safari, So Good!* New York,
N.Y.: Random House, 2011.

ON THE WEB
Learning more about
antelopes is as easy as 1, 2, 3.

1. Go to www.factsurfer.com.

2. Enter "antelopes" into the search box.

3. Click the "Surf" button and you will see a
   list of related Web sites.

With factsurfer.com, finding more information
is just a click away.

Index

The images in this book are reproduced through the courtesy of: Villiers Steyn, front cover;
Juan Martinez, p. 5 (small); Hoberman Collection/ SuperStock, p. 5; Sasha Gusov/ Age
Fotostock, p. 7; Mhpiper, p. 9; Johan Swanepoel/ Age Fotostock, p. 11; Laurent Geslin/
Biosphoto, p. 13; Ivan Kuzmin/ Age Fotostock, p. 15; Anna Omelchenko, p. 17; Christian
Hutter/ imag/ Age Fotostock, p. 19; John Devries/ Age Fotostock, p. 21.